CHOOSE TO

BECOME

A guide to cultivating self-awareness and healing so you can become the best version of you

LINDSEY CACY

CONCRETE ROSE
PUBLISHING

Published by Concrete Rose Publishing

ISBN 978-1-7368969-0-7

For Kalvin and Zakaria.
Thank you both for saving my life and for
being my greatest teachers. I love you.

Contents

INTRODUCTION

Take a Deep Breath

"But still, like air, I'll rise" –Maya Angelou

The fact that you are reading this book is somewhat of a miracle. And not just because there are millions of other self-help books that you could've grabbed. I say that this book is miraculous because based on statistics and the various experiences I've walked through in my life; I probably shouldn't have lived long enough to write it.

I'll never forget the morning of November 20, 2008: I woke up early, before my then two-year-old son, and immediately heard rain falling. I snuggled deeper into the comforter that covered my little bed and smiled; thoroughly enjoying the sound of rainwater pitter-pattering on the rooftop. After a few moments I got up and wandered into the kitchen to make some coffee. As the coffee brewed, I grabbed my hoodie and a cigarette, and once my coffee was done, I headed outside to my front porch.

It was still raining lightly and dark, so I sat near my doorway, trying to stay out of the rain's reach. Although I have not smoked in many years, I can still remember the satisfaction I felt taking that first drag of my first cigarette of the day. I gazed down my driveway, blinking a few stray raindrops out of my eyes and saw the neighbor's cat walking up to me.

"Aww, love, you should be inside," I murmured as I pet her damp fur. As if on cue she slinked past me to sit inside my entryway as she sometimes did. I smiled and shook my head, turning my attention back to the rain. I've always liked rainy mornings, but this morning felt uniquely calming and purifying; almost hypnotic. As I stared into the mist, I had a singular thought that was so profound that it filled my entire being with a deep sense of gratitude and emotion.

I made it.

Then the tears came, mixing with the cool, misty rain. Suddenly, I wasn't cold or mad that my cigarette had been ruined by the wet air outside. I was filled with a sense of awe so deep, that it was palpable. These were the first moments of my twenty-fifth birthday and my first, conscious spiritual experience.

There are so many reasons why I wanted to write this book, and for many years I knew I would eventually write it. I just didn't have the context or self-awareness in those earlier years to successfully put my experiences into cohesive stories that would help someone else. Shit, I could barely help myself; most of my twenties were spent simply *surviving*. And, even after the literal survival, I was left to survive the internal turmoil that plagued me up until a few years ago.

My life was disconnected from conception. My mother used heroine throughout her entire pregnancy with me, so I was born fighting for my life and without the benefit of sobriety. My early childhood was like an emotional boot camp; harshly but successfully establishing unhealthy conditioning, and feelings of unworthiness based on the sexual, physical and emotional abuse I experienced during those early years.

9

I stumbled blindly through most of my early adult years seeking external validation in the unhealthiest of ways. I searched for my value in individuals who also didn't know their worth. I've unconsciously played out past traumas in friendships, romantic relationships and even with family. I turned to drugs to cope with the constant pain and angst I felt within myself.

Even after getting off drugs in 2004, I was still living a life of dissatisfaction, anxiety and addictive tendencies. You see, just getting off drugs didn't heal the wounds or create immediate growth. I had to take a few more big blows before finally surrendering and looking at all my shit.

In 2014, I discovered Yoga after an unexpected surgery due to some major health issues I was facing, so I was required to stop my normal exercise routine. My doctor suggested I try yoga and I told her I'd look into it. I'd heard of it but never practiced or even seen it done before. Little did I know at the time that this would become a major catalyst into my healing journey.

When I first began practicing, I would watch yoga videos on YouTube and follow along as best I could. I did this for two reasons – first off, I couldn't afford to attend a studio or gym and lastly, because I was too self-conscious to try my hand at it in front of anyone.

Initially, I would get frustrated with the beginner poses that I couldn't seem to achieve. My breath would be ragged, and I would become exasperated because I couldn't follow the breath cues that the teacher on the video was demonstrating. Anytime I would fall out of a pose I would internally beat myself up. The teachers made it look so easy and I felt like I looked like a wounded flamingo. I did, however, keep going back to the same video until I felt like I had mastered it. And I did usually feel just a teensy bit more centered by the last few minutes of the online class.

I realize now that those moments of getting frustrated on the mat; those moments of resistance, were mirroring the moments I would get frustrated off the mat. They were the places where my ego was showing itself. Those moments on the mat were showing me (whether I wanted to see it or not) my emotional blind spots and unhealthy patterns of behavior. When I would get my breathing wrong or fall out of a pose for the eighth time, I would inwardly shame myself – mostly unconsciously at first. I was doing the exact same thing when I would make a mistake at work or say the wrong thing in a social setting. The scary part was that I lived so many years doing it and wasn't even aware of it.

It wasn't until I decided to do yoga teacher training in 2016 that I became consciously aware of the connection between my reactions on the mat and my reactions in everyday life. Sure, I knew that Yoga was making me feel good and made me feel a bit calmer, but I didn't fully understand how much Yoga was enlightening me emotionally and spiritually until 2016. We will dive more into this later in the book, but for now, I will just say that my Yoga practice allowed me a safe space to explore my shit and discover myself. It provided me with the most powerful gift – self-awareness. Self-awareness is not something we arrive at; it is, just like yoga, a practice. We are multifaceted beings, always learning, growing and expanding. With every new experience, we gain a broader perspective of ourselves and the world we live in. This is why self-awareness must be a conscious choice and nurtured through consistent check-ins with ourselves.

As I am writing this, I feel a similar sense of awe and gratitude to what I felt on my twenty-fifth birthday.

The journey of creating this book has been cathartic, sacred and hard; but mostly, it's been incredibly healing.

During the process of writing this book, I also remembered that this is the second book I've written. The first book was called *That's the Way Life Goes* and I wrote it in fourth grade.

No, this wasn't an elementary school writing project; I wrote it (and illustrated it, thank you very much) because I wanted to experience being an author. I was always an avid reader and I wanted to try my hand at writing my own story. I remember taking it in to my teacher and seeing her face - she was puzzled because this wasn't an assignment she had given, and most kids don't just roll up into class with a completed manuscript. I asked her if she could bind it for me, and she did.

The book was about a woman who, throughout her day, had a series of unfortunate events occur: she spilled her coffee all over herself, got caught outside in the rain, and when she got home, her poodle (named Sunny) had shit all over her carpet. The book ends with her accepting that it was a bad day, cuddling with her misbehaving pooch and saying the final line of the book which was "well, that's just the way life goes!"

In some ways that book was a prerequisite to this one. Sure, it was an amateur product and I was only nine, but the message of accepting what we cannot change and cultivating the ability to reframe negative situations, is uncannily similar to many of the concepts I present in this book.

The main theme of this book is unpacking the power of choice and helping you understand that you, not your life circumstances, get to choose who you become. My intention with this book is to help you realize how worthy you are of healing and feeling good in your life. The tools in this book will support you even after you finish the book; you can revisit the journal prompts and mantras as your life changes and shifts.

In yoga, we sometimes end classes with the Sanskrit greeting, *Namaste*, which translates to "The light in me sees and honors the light in you" So, with that being said, *Namaste*; I bow to you in reverence for your decision to dive deep with me and for choosing to do the work necessary to become the person you've always wanted to be. I am so glad you're here.

CHAPTER ONE

Self-Awareness is Your Superpower

"The most important conversations you'll ever have are the ones you'll have with yourself." — David Goggins

When I started writing this book it was the summer of 2019 and it was a much simpler time—and by simpler, I mean life before the pandemic. By the time this book comes out, I am hoping that the whole Covid-19 pandemic situation is more under control than it is now. I had originally decided to release this book in the Summer of 2020, but life had other plans.

Life and her damn plans, right?

I mean, we spend so much of our lives trying to control every aspect of it and life will just look at our plans and snicker, "oh you silly human, don't you know you're not the one running the show?" We buy pretty planners and have all the productivity apps on our cell phones to keep us on track for our hopes and dreams and our lives in general. In our minds, we think *if I plan out every single detail just right, things will go as planned.*

Now here we sit in a collective shit-show realizing how little control we truly have over our external world. We have each been affected in different ways by the pandemic and increased social tension— some more horrific than others. Some of us have lost jobs, some have lost loved ones, but all of us, at some point during this pandemic, have lost our normal access to social interactions. We have fewer activities outside of the home which means we are spending much more time with ourselves. Spending time by ourselves and with our thoughts can be a scary place, especially if you are someone who hasn't spent a lot of time with yourself.

In my early adulthood, I hated being by myself – I mean, I would get such bad anxiety that I had to go to someone's house or even go to the mall just to be around others and not be alone with my thoughts. I know now that was because my mind was a place filled with bad memories, unprocessed trauma, and incredibly low self-worth.

Because the home I grew up in was emotionally and psychologically abusive, I carry with me those old wounds, and they would get triggered by experiences that remind me of situations during that time. Because I didn't have the language or context of those things, I just felt like something was wrong with me because I seemed so much more reactive and sensitive than everyone around me. Let me give you an example.

When I was young, my biological mother, who was addicted to heroine, would often leave my brother and me unattended. I vividly remember being a small child at home alone with my brother, and we would look for our mother around the house. When we didn't find her, we would often go outside to try and find her – sometimes at night.

At night, by ourselves.

We were only four and five years old. Sometimes our neighbors would walk us back to our apartment and other times my brother and I would find our own way home. After a couple of years of this, we ended up in foster care because of my mother's inability to take care of us. I remember the police coming to remove us from the home, and although I did not know exactly what was going on, I didn't feel afraid to go with the officers. As a mother now who knows how intuitive children can be, I can look back and know that even though I didn't have the full grasp of what was happening around me, I had the subtle awareness that I was not safe.

We were then taken to a place where they temporarily kept foster children who have been recently removed from their home but don't yet have a place to go – I remember it was called "The Dependent Unit," and the only memory I have of that night was the super dope Jellies shoes one of the ladies that worked there gave me. (Side note for the ladies: if you've never heard of or seen Jellies, Google them, they are so eighties and so cute!)

The important gem of wisdom that I really want you to grasp is that in those moments, I didn't have awareness that lifelong abandonment issues were being created. I had absolutely no idea that what I was living in was wrong because I didn't know anything different.

You see, context is such an important ingredient for so many things in life. When we have a better understanding of something, we can heal it and create real change in our lives. But first we have to be willing to look at it.

And this, my friend, brings us back to our ability (or inability) to sit with ourselves. I believe the most important opinion in our lives is the opinion we have of ourselves – how do you feel about yourself when you are by yourself? I don't mean by yourself scrolling through Instagram or watching TV either. I mean being solo in a quiet space with none of your usual vices or distractions.

Do you ever spend undivided time with yourself? Where does your mind go?

I want you to pause reading for a moment to really consider these questions – and really be honest with yourself about it. The nice thing about reading a personal-development book is that it is just that – *personal*. So, take full advantage of this moment and allow yourself to think about this – and try to do so without too much judgment; be as objective (and honest!) as you can.

What changed my ability to spend time alone without distractions was doing just that – spending time alone without distraction. That sounds easy, right?

Nah.

Not when you've spent years avoiding that very activity.

My conscious journey to self-reflection and self-assessment began in early 2016. I had just discovered spirituality that resonated with me when my brother, Joshua, showed me a YouTube show called *Buddha at the Gas Pump*. On this show, the host would interview spiritual teachers and sometimes even some regular people who have had profound spiritual awakenings. I didn't know what a spiritual awakening was when I started watching it. To be honest, I mostly started watching it to feel closer to my brother who had recently been diagnosed with stage four pancreatic cancer (more on this later.) Also, he was so pumped up about it that I became intrigued.

I knew within the first few moments of the first episode that this was something I needed to pursue. I began listening daily and although the language was new, the experiences they were describing resonated on a very deep level. I didn't know exactly what a spiritual awakening was but I knew intuitively that it was something I needed to understand so I could feel better in my life. The more I listened, the more I realized that I'd had some spiritual experiences in my life already. After a few months, I discovered Abraham Hicks and they really spoke to me and deepened my spiritual connection and feelings of spiritual guidance.

Despite my affinity for some pretty woo-woo sounding stuff, I was raised very religiously. I grew up going to a Baptist church on some Sundays and I read the bible often – like without anyone telling me to do so. The thirst for spiritual knowledge and connection was already there and Christianity was my entry point. I vividly remember sitting alone in my room praying and talking with God – as early as age five. Perhaps it was because the pastor referred to him as father and us as his children, which would be very appealing to a little girl with no parents. Either way, I felt connected and safe when I thought of God.

Although religion didn't resonate with me in the same way that spirituality does, the idea of being connected to something bigger than myself always spoke to me; I *felt* it. But through many negative life experiences, I lost that feeling of connection and moreover, I lost that feeling of trust. So eventually, I stopped creating those quiet moments to connect.

Between the previous foundations of prayer, Abraham Hicks repeatedly telling me to meditate daily to feel good, and my yoga teacher training in 2016, I finally found myself craving alone time to process and contemplate my life and feelings. I began to look forward to being alone with my thoughts and myself. As someone who consumed drugs as a way to not feel all the pain buried within, this was *huge*. This is how I know that this stuff works, and this is also why I know that you, too, can access peace through self-reflection. We cannot heal what we are not willing to look at. In this chapter we will look at some tools to help you on your journey to increasing your self-awareness.

I am a Yoga teacher, and as I mentioned in the introduction, my journey to this practice was unconventional to say the least. I also wasn't raised in a home where mindfulness was never mentioned, so I almost felt like yoga and meditation found me.

Sometimes things become so suffocating that you have nowhere to go but inward. When hardships occur, it's easy to feel swallowed up by your life as opposed to be the one living and dare I say... creating it. Then, as we focus on the unwanted situation, we keep the emotional train rushing in that direction, creating other unwanted situations because the energy we are broadcasting and the thoughts we are thinking are now aligned with things not going our way. Often, we begin to skip out on self-care and pick up more unhealthy habits (drinking, overeating, smoking, etc.) during these stressful times.

When bad things happen, having spiritual practice is crucial. Checking in with yourself through stillness and reflection is the best way to nourish our soul and spirit.

But often we try to go around or jump over uncomfortable situations to avoid going through the things that make us squirm. This is what creates that unconscious loop of old behavior and patterns - this is what makes us feel overly anxious and overwhelmed by life. Well, this just in: life is full of things that might make you uncomfortable. Things are going to happen that upset you, trigger you, or make you doubt yourself.

Mindfulness practices show us the areas we need to grow or heal in.

Conscious breathing and movement have been the most effective tools for me to get in touch with myself. While meditation and Yoga don't take away the trigger, these practices do create some space between the trigger and the old ways of reacting. I've learned to observe this alchemy in real time - to feel that familiar, uncomfortable feeling arise but then becoming a witness to it instead of regurgitating practiced reactions.

This takes practice of course which is why it is called a meditation *practice* or a Yoga *practice*. In that pause and shift from reaction to introspection, I find this sweet spot of silence and relief. I can be separate from the issue so that I can understand it and move through it. When we move through something, we can move past it.

Simple Meditation Instructions:

Sit in a quiet area where you are likely to not be disturbed for a while. This is part of why I do it first thing in the morning. Set a timer on your phone for 15 minutes, then turn your phone volume off.

Close your eyes and begin to deepen your breath. For me, it helps to inhale for a count of 4 then exhale for a count of four. The more you practice the deeper and steadier your breath will become. When your mind wanders (and it will... often at first) gently, and without judgment, bring your attention back to your breath.

When your timer goes off, if you feel called to, you can write about the experience or whatever comes up for you. You are most aligned with your highest self immediately after meditation so it can be a powerful time to journal and set intentions for your day and beyond.

CHAPTER TWO

What are You Choosing?

"I am not what happened to me, I am what I choose to become." –C.G. Yung

I discovered this Carl Yung quote several years ago and although it resonated on some level back then, it didn't become a universal truth for me until after some tumultuous life experience hit me upside the head. As my father used to say, "the hard-headed always have to feel it to believe it."

If there is only one concept that you take from this book, I hope it is this one: **we get to decide who we become.** I believe so strongly in the idea behind the quote that I got it tattooed on my arm so I could be reminded of it daily. I know from my own life experience that we are resilient beings and powerful creators. I didn't know this truth until I gained some self-awareness and that is what I want to emphasize in this chapter: we can decide at any point in our lives to shift out of negative ways of living and step into our unique greatness. We just need to figure out who we are first – and that means not being afraid to really look at ourselves as well as the choices we've made in life that have brought us here, to this moment.

I was the girl who believed that life was happening *to* her; I felt that I had very little control over most of what occurred in my life. Especially during my early childhood years, things always felt out of my control. I was placed in foster care at an early age due to my biological mother's heroin addiction. My father, who was born in 1918, didn't have the space to keep my brother and I and was deemed "too old" to take on two toddlers. Of course, I don't remember many of the details from those years, but I do know from the child development classes I took in college that just because the memories are foggy doesn't mean the signature of those experiences doesn't live within me.

As we begin to exit the autopilot style of living and fully commit to our lives, we also begin to understand the power of our choices. Everything we do, every action we take, begins with a choice. We can choose to have the oatmeal and fruit instead of the donut for breakfast. We can choose to leave the relationship where our partner continues to demonstrate that they don't value us. You can choose to go to counseling or reach out to a trusted friend instead of turning to drugs to numb your pain.

Depending on where you are in your life and the choices you've been making, this may bring up feelings of resistance within you. You may be feeling frustrated, attacked or in disbelief by what I'm proposing. Perhaps you're thinking *I didn't choose to be in this situation/relationship/illness/job/etc.* I'm not saying you chose the hardships in your life. I'm not saying you are wrong or bad for your past choices. I *am* saying that you get to choose what your life looks like moving forward. I am saying this to empower you to become the master of your fate and an active participant in the creation of your beautiful future.

I can't talk about the power of choice without sharing my addiction story. I also share this because I think we all struggle with addiction in some form – maybe for you its food, or external validation, or perhaps it is also drugs, like mine was. We will talk more about the logistics of changing unhealthy habits in the *New Habit, Who Dis?* chapter. For the purpose of this chapter, I share this story in hopes that it will help you understand the undeniable power of choice.

I remember being 20 years old and sitting in the bathtub sobbing on Christmas morning. My boyfriend, who I was living with at the time, had left to visit his family for Christmas and I had chosen to stay home. Holidays have always been particularly hard for me due to losing my parents when I was a child. I also didn't really have anywhere else to be because of the strained relationship with my adoptive family during those years.

But that wasn't why I was crying in a bathtub on Christmas morning. I was crying because there was a syringe of methamphetamines sitting on the counter and I didn't know how to inject myself with it. I was crying because I couldn't get high.

When I was 19, one of my first boyfriends had introduced me to the drug. As soon as I tried it, I liked the way I felt on it. I had an extremely sheltered childhood after the age of 5, so when I turned 18 and was on my own, I had very little knowledge of the world and my social skills were essentially nonexistent. The drug gave me a false sense of bravery and an openness in social settings that I had never known. When I was high, I felt less self-conscious about my social awkwardness. I was immediately hooked.

Being high also allowed me to temporarily forget the inner turmoil I often felt, and it helped me escape the feeling that I was alone in the world. I know now that those feelings of turmoil were attributed to years of unprocessed trauma and that the drug wasn't helping release that trauma, it was only delaying the inevitable emotional and spiritual breakdown.

I started smoking the drug and then snorting it. Towards the end, I was having the drug administered intravenously. I never learned how to inject myself, which explains the manic morning in the tub. I had been doing the drug intravenously for a couple months at this point but had only allowed my boyfriend at the time to inject me. In hindsight, what a blessing.

It wasn't long after that relationship when I got sober. I cringe even referring to the situation as a relationship because that was the furthest thing from what it was. It was more like a convenient place to live coupled with a mutual affinity for the same substance.

I know now that those pivotal moments were my rock bottom experiences; the sequence of events that were undeniable proof that things were out of control. Those moments created an awareness in me about how bad things had really gotten and this allowed my perspective to slowly shift. One of the final signs for me was when I began having dreams (on the nights that I slept) that I had died. Like, I would see myself in a casket in my dreams. I began to honestly believe that I would not live past twenty-five if I continued on this destructive path. This explains that emotional experience in the rain on the morning of my twenty-fifth birthday. There was a time when I genuinely wasn't sure if I'd arrive at that milestone.

When I stopped using, I didn't go to rehab. Over the two years that I used the drug heavily, I would watch people's families trying to send them to rehabs and detox centers. I had watched so many people go to these rehabs and then pop back up on the scene months later to buy some drugs. I didn't have parental guidance, nor did I have family support. The difference for me, and the point I am trying to make here is that one day, I decided.

This is how I know that everything – and I mean *everything* – is a choice. Therefore, I so adamantly suggest this concept to you. This isn't something I read about in a book or took a class on - this is my experience. There were many moments of wanting to stop, of telling myself this was the last shot or bump or bowl. But when I was truly ready to create a different life for myself, I decided and then I acted.

In total, I did meth for a little over two years, but it felt like a lifetime because of all the things I experienced in that short time. I saw the worst in people: I was punched in the face by two different boyfriends more than once, I watched a mother hitting a meth pipe while breastfeeding her baby, I saw countless people rob their families blind to support their drug habit. I just couldn't stay in a world like that for long.

I am in no way insinuating that I felt that I was better than any of my peers. And I do strongly believe that everyone is different and that some people will need outside support to get them to the other side of addiction. Whatever gets you out of addiction is a win in my opinion. I think because I never had that family support during those years, I knew that no one was coming to save me or to offer to put me through a rehab program. I was either going to find a way out myself or follow in the footsteps of my mother who overdosed.

I knew that a life of drugs wasn't going to be my whole life – even when I was actively getting high. I remember getting teased by fellow addicts because I would often say, "I'm not doing this forever, I'm just doing it right now." Which, for the record, EVERY drug addict says. But I knew on a deeper level that my life was going to be bigger, better and just different. I just got lost for a while.

After the trauma of my childhood, after the abuse in relationships by men who claimed to love me, after all the loss and darkness, I knew on a soul level that there had to be more. But everyone around me said that once people start shooting up, they never get sober. Well, a few months after getting sober, I got *the letters* tattooed on my back – this stands for Living Proof. I am living proof that you can change, that you can fucking decide and that is one of your greatest superpowers.

Two years after getting sober, I gave birth to my first son and decided to get my GED and take some classes at my local community college. When my son was 6 months old, I received my GED and I took my first college class at 24 years old. My original intention was to receive a certificate to become a drug counselor. I quickly realized in my first counseling class, that this was not the path for me. After hearing about other people's journeys to sobriety, I realized how unique my situation was. I never went to rehab. The few Narcotics Anonymous meetings I did go to, I didn't like simply because the philosophy was if you go out and get high, you can just come back and they will accept you with open arms.

For me, there couldn't be that option of slipping up knowing I would be welcomed back. I know plenty of people who have benefited from NA so I know the program works for people; I just knew for myself that I could not undo the original choice of *no more*. I had to stand firm in that decision, come hell or high water.

I didn't have the language or life experience at that time to fully understand why I couldn't help people get clean using the methods I was being introduced to. I do remember knowing internally that my situation was unique and that getting sober was a very personal and intimate decision that could only be lasting if a person was ready to quit for themselves.

Acknowledge Your Past Choices

We've all fucked up before; we have all done things we are not proud of. Every single person on this earth has made choices that disrupted their path. But, the beautiful thing about making poor choices is that we can, 1. learn from them and, 2. make different choices moving forward. It is never too late to change your reality through changing the choices you make each day. Change is cumulative so even if we do not see immediate results from our smaller changes, we are still actively participating in becoming our best selves. Over time, you will see how your reality is shifting for the better.

One thing to point out here is the difference between acknowledging your past choices and beating yourself up for choices that have already been made. What is done is done and no matter how much we'd like to, we cannot change the past. Our job in these situations is to hold ourselves accountable so that we can do things differently in the future. When we consciously look at our not-so-cute or toxic traits, we can understand how our actions affect others and how they even affect us. This creates self-awareness. This creates empathy. I believe if each of us does the inner work to create more empathy and self-awareness, the world would become better.

It is important to take a real, honest look at our past choices (even when it's uncomfortable) so that we can understand how they've affected our life now. But look back with gratitude and respect for what you've learned from them, not with regret or shame. Every single decision we've made, every stumble and detour, has taught us something incredibly valuable.

Journal Prompts

What is a choice you've made recently that affected your life in a negative way? (Be detailed here – and remember – no shaming yourself! You are just identifying the decision and writing out the situation in detail.)

Looking at the decision and its aftermath objectively, what is at least one thing that you can take away from the experience that you learned? (The more you can reframe it, the better, so dig deep here. Don't get lost in the choice, look at what you've learned from it.)

When faced with a similar situation in the future, how can you make a different, more informed choice to enhance the outcome of the situation? List three ways you can do things differently moving forward.

Suggested Mantras

I acknowledge my past choices with accountability and forgiveness.

My past choices do not define who I am moving forward.

I forgive myself for unhealthy choices I've made in the past.

CHAPTER THREE

New Habit, Who Dis?

"Depending on what they are, our habits will either make us or break us. We become what we repeatedly do." —*Sean Covey*

Whether you are aware of it or not, your daily habits have the power to shape your entire life. Everything that you do in your daily life now has a beginning - a time when you started doing the activity that is now part of your daily routine. When we do something repeatedly for any length of time, it eventually becomes habitual.

Our habits typically fall within one of two categories: healthy or unhealthy, and productive or unproductive. When we want to create lasting change in our lives, we have to be really honest about the things that we do each day.

How aware are you of your day-to-day habits?

With so much information in front of our faces about how to get healthy, get rich, or create a life you really like, it is preposterous to say we don't know what we need to do in order to change. It's as easy as picking up your phone (which, let's be real, is probably in your hand 80% of the time) and searching for the answer. You will instantly be given answers and, in most cases, step-by-step instructions on how to do the thing.

The issue isn't a lack of information – the issue is our lack of self-awareness, discipline and a clear understanding of why we want what we want.

We have the best of intentions and are genuinely excited about the new habit. We know it will help us feel better or get what we want in life. We may even start doing the new thing for a few days, but then, at the first sign of inconvenience or after one bad day, we make excuses for why we started missing days. Once we begin slacking on the routine for days at a time, we eventually fall off the wagon.

Think back to a time when you heard about some new habit that was in alignment with where you wanted your life to go: you lit up and decided this was perfect for you and would help you get you back on track. Maybe it was a new workout, or a new diet - whatever it was - you woke up the very next day and wholeheartedly did the new thing.

You may have done it for an entire week or even two, but then the next thing you know, something happened that threw you off your routine and you missed a day. Then you miss another day. And the cycle continues. Now, cue the shame-storm - you begin to beat yourself up internally and make yourself feel worse than you did before you even found out about the new habit you embarked on. Or, maybe you see other people keeping up on their habits and you start to attack your own worth by allowing feelings of self-loathing to steep in your being.

We have all been there. We have all set out to complete a goal or new habit, and then fell off a few days or a few months later. Just think back to the endless New Year's resolutions that were fully forgotten by February 5th.

As with most things in life, there is a flip side to habits. The other side of choosing healthy habits, is understanding and acknowledging our unhealthy habits. These unhealthy habits are things we have done so many times that they too became automatic. These things can be as simple as having a Coca-Cola every afternoon or as extreme as being dependent on drugs to get through your day.

So, how the hell do we end the cycle of self-destruction and live our best, healthy-habit-having lives you may ask. It's actually really simple. Creating healthy habits is about realizing **why** you want to make the change, and then choosing yourself again and again.

Notice that I did not say it's *easy* - I said it's *simple*.

There are a million new habits you could adopt that could completely change your life. You probably have some ideas swirling in your head of things to improve your life.

The first thing I want you to do is to drop the "should". *I should* is not a reason to change. Every time I stopped getting high because I felt like I *should*, I always found myself getting high a week or so later. It wasn't until I craved sobriety and all the beautiful gifts that I intuitively knew came with it, that I quit once and for all.

According to Healthline.com, it takes about 66 days for a behavior to become automatic. For me personally, I notice the shift within thirty days – which may sound like a long time in our instant gratification society. But, when you think of how many months or years you've spent unconsciously (or consciously) creating some of your existing habits, you wouldn't think so.

I am going to break this down into steps you can use to create your own plan of action, and so that you can easily refer back to this section whenever you want to create another new, healthy change in your life. Know that you can do this! The power is yours, and I believe in you.

Make Your Why Your Foundation

The first step is to confirm why you want to make this change in your life. Maybe you want to create a body you are happy with, so the habit you want to create is working out and eating healthily. Or perhaps you need to calm down and stop being so stressed, so you want to start a meditation and/or yoga practice. Maybe you want to write a book or start a blog, so you need to create a daily writing habit. Once you establish the habit you wish to create or the bad habit you want to discontinue, you must really get clear on **why** you want this change. The initial excitement will fade (as we all know from experience), so you will need that deeper motivation to push through the times when you just don't feel like doing the things you know you need to do. You can write your why down in a journal or you can try the method I often use, which is writing in the notes of my phone. We all have cell phones, and we all spend an unspeakable amount of time staring at them, so why not have this sacred information there?

Here is an example of a powerful Why Statement:

Habit I want to incorporate: *Exercising for 30 minutes every day.*

My why: *I am going to exercise every day for thirty minutes because I want to have more energy and build a healthier, stronger body. I want to feel good in the clothes I am wearing, and I want to feel good about myself by making this commitment to myself a habit. I want to feel good about how I look, and I want to keep my body healthy through movement.*

Your why statement must be specific to you and how you want to feel. This is what you will come back to when you aren't feeling motivated to continue with the new activity.

Keeping it Real(istic)

The other place where we screw ourselves over is by getting TOO excited and trying to take on more than one habit at a time. We will get all stoked and in that wonder woman/superman mode and be like "bro, I got this and I'm also gonna stop eating meat and dairy and gluten while I build this brand-new weekly exercise habit." While I appreciate the excitement and borderline blind belief in self, I know from experience that this is not realistic and will usually lead to overwhelm, burn out and ultimately failure. And the more we fail; the more we tend to build negative momentum and just spiral into that dark place of excessive Netflix and self-judgment. Failure does serve us, but if we are not also learning from those failures, we will just repeat the cycle until we get the lesson.

I suggest that you just pick one to begin with. As we now know, it can take about 66 days to make a habit automatic. Depending on the habit I will give it anywhere from thirty days to twelve weeks.

Let's say you want to start a meditation practice – you will wake up 15-30 minutes earlier than you normally do so you can sit down and breathe for 15 minutes before you do anything else. Do this for 10 days, and I promise you will notice a shift in your reactions and emotions; do it for 30 days and it will become a habit. Once you feel like you've mastered one and want to build on your routine, then you can make changes and add things in.

Stacks on Stacks on Stacks

Ok, so you now have been meditating for a month and you are feeling yourself (as you should be.) What you are feeling is more like your best self. From this space of achievement and positive momentum, you can now add on a new habit. This is referred to as *habit stacking* – when you master one, you can build on that momentum to create more positive change. The best way to do this is to find something that complements our existing habits – like maybe a gratitude practice, journaling, or yoga. For this example, we will add 20 minutes of exercise to the already existing meditation practice.

The thirty-day cycle will start over and you'll do your normal 15 minutes of meditation and then immediately do 20 minutes of exercise. Tips to make this easier would be to make sure you are getting at least 7-8 hours of sleep the night before, make sure your workout clothes are out and ready to go (maybe even sleep in them!), and only allow yourself to watch your favorite show while you are on the treadmill. Find what motivates you and makes this initial transition process easier—you are much more likely to stick with it if it's convenient or enticing.

It can be as simple as 50 squats, 50 sit ups and some pushups. START SMALL. Remember, keeping it realistic and manageable is going to make it feel less daunting – especially on day seventeen.

Enroll an Accountability Buddy

This is one of my favorites! I for sure had a couple accountability buddies (one of which was my Instagram stories) to ensure I was getting my word counts in for this book. If you are a fellow procrastinator (hey), this will work wonders for you. Knowing that someone is going to be checking in with you about your progress on the new habit will add that supportive pressure that some of us need to buckle down. And remember, it's temporary! Once you are doing your new activity for a few weeks, it will become automatic.

An accountability buddy doubles as a sounding board/support system when you feel like you are falling off or can't continue. They can cheer you on or give you the sometimes hard-to-hear (but loving and honest) reminder that you are choosing not to prioritize your new, healthier way of life. I know for me this was always hard because I was already worried about what people thought of me, so admitting my failed attempts at something felt gut-wrenching. But sometimes we need that extra kick in the pants to get focused and be reminded that we get to choose. The other benefit is gaining the realization that we all have moments of failure and triumph – no one is perfect or immune to regressing from time to time. We are all just hanging out together on this gigantic, spinning planet trying to hold our shit together and have more good days than bad. Give yourself some grace.

Now, it's time for you to take an honest look at your habits. A big reason I share my experiences so vulnerably is because I want you to get vulnerable with yourself about what isn't working anymore in your life. That truly is the first step – taking extreme ownership of the choices we've made and making the changes we know deep down with help us feel better. Look at these questions from an angle of compassion and maybe even excitement if you can muster it. Excitement that you are not a bad person and not wrong for your poor choices – you just weren't ready yet. And that is ok.

Don't beat yourself up or judge yourself too much. In every moment we get to *decide* how we want to show up, so show up for yourself now by taking some time to answer these questions. Allow these to provide you with some clarity and be the catalyst for you to step into your best self.

These are questions you can use again and again throughout the year to reassess and realign – this is not a one-time exercise!

Journal Prompts:

What are the habits that you most want to incorporate into your daily or weekly routine?

What are the benefits you will gain from starting this new habit? *(I.e., how will you feel about yourself when you accomplish this? Make it real – you really want to feel this – you will be referring to this when the going gets tough.)*

What reminders and rewards are you going to have in place to ensure your success?

What are the habits or routines that make you feel bad about yourself?

CHAPTER FOUR

Kick Your Inner Critic to the Curb

"Your inner critic is simply a part of you that needs more self-love." —Amy Leigh Mercree

Although this is obviously not the first chapter of the book, I wrote this chapter first. I did this because my inner critic was all up in my face with that *who do you think you are to write this book?* energy.

Not today, Satan.

Instead of meekly submitting to self-doubt and forfeiting my dream, I sat with that question and spent some time examining all the reasons why *I am* meant to write this book. After I was able to tune out the inner critic's noise and tune into that quiet knowing within me, it was quite obvious what to do. I had to push past the fear and do it anyway, because in my heart and soul, I feel called to write this book. So, the fact that you have this book in your hands is additional proof that your inner critic is not someone you should be consulting with when you want to do something new or challenging in your life.

Most of us are familiar with the reoccurring thoughts of self-doubt that leave us questioning our ideas and, sometimes, even our worth. It can show up in many scenarios of our lives: when we are trying something new, looking in the mirror, or setting bigger goals for ourselves. Unchecked, this terrible cancer can spread, and we are soon playing so small that we don't recognize ourselves or our lives.

This can also come up in our closest, most trusted relationships and cause us to question everything. I lost relationships because I was constantly listening to my negative internal narrative that questioned everything about the relationship that I was in. Had I understood during those times that the real issue was my own feelings of insecurity and unworthiness; I could've done the work then to change the internal messaging I was unconsciously accepting as fact. But as the great Maya Angelou said, when we know better, we do better.

Here is a recent, and somewhat embarrassing example from my own life: a few months ago, a past mentor of mine who always gets back to me quickly when I text her, didn't text me back for few days. By day three, these are the thoughts that began to creep in:

"She's probably mad at you for always being so busy..."

"Remember that one time she wanted to hang out a couple months ago and you said you couldn't because you needed some time to unwind? She probably resents you now because you didn't make time for her."

I'll admit – my inner critic can be a bit (well, completely) dramatic. But I think we can all agree that this inner voice can be a bit of an asshole at times. Once I was able to take a step back and realize how negative those thoughts were, I was able to chill out and assume the best instead of the worst. *She is also super busy*, I thought, *I'll check back in next week.*

In the past, this would've eaten away at me until I'd begun to believe it. Or worse, imagine if I would've created a story around this imaginary scenario that my mind had presented and asked her about it, being it all defensive! I am not proud to admit I have done that exact thing in past relationships. So. Dumb. Thank goodness for the growth. Now that I have cultivated more self-awareness and understand that this inner critic character cannot always be trusted, I can pause to check in with my rational mind before spiraling down that rabbit hole I used to spend a lot of time exploring.

Also, in case you're curious, my friend got back to me by day four - she let me know she had also been super busy and that she desperately wanted to hang out. Relationship catastrophe avoided.

Disclaimer: Before we dive all the way in – we *all* have an inner critic. We all have that little voice in our mind that sometimes makes us question ourselves and others. You'll have an epic idea, get all fired up about the new project, and then you hear that faint voice say, *"who are YOU to do that?"* Some people's inner critic will be louder or visit more frequently than others' but having that inner voice of self-doubt is a universal trait. To kick self-doubt to the metaphorical curb, we must first understand what it is and where it comes from.

But where *does* this come from? Why do we have this seemingly built-in hater in our head?

This voice was formed for most of us in our childhood by anyone who was close to us that ever said something that was critical, mean or judgmental – even our own parents. When they would tell us things that made us feel less than (whether it was intentional, or not), we internalized it without realizing the havoc it would wreak later on our lives.

In childhood, this voice was helped along by some of our peers and teachers, but as adults, it often looks like romantic partners reaffirming our existing fears or creating new insecurities. The more we hear the same kinds of things about ourselves, the more they become a belief and feel true to us. The more we feel that something is true about us, or is "just who we are," the more we shrink to fit what we think others will be more comfortable with, and play small in our lives.

If you were chastised daily for every little mistake you made as a kid by someone close to you, I'd be willing to bet that when you try something new in your life now, and don't get it exactly right, your initial thought or words to your yourself are probably, *"ugh, I am so stupid!"*

I am not saying our parents or the adults in our lives were terrible people and deliberately said things to scar us for the long term. I don't even fully blame the partners we've had in adulthood for helping create this inner critic – we have to remember that people can only offer us what is within them. I honestly believe the adults in our lives were doing the best they could at that time. If our parents weren't actively working through their own trauma, there is no way they could parent us in a way that was 100% conscious, wholehearted and without unhealthy messaging. It is unfair to expect one or two adults to have the capacity to teach us *everything* we need to know about becoming a healthy, thriving adult. As a parent now, I understand this and have so much more compassion for the woman that raised me.

Judgement + Comparison

The only reason our inner dialogue should begin with the question *"who am I to ...?"* is if that last word is judge:

"who am I to judge?"

When we judge others, we are robbing ourselves of unconditional connection and love. Our judgments of others come from one of two places: love or fear. When we make judgments from a place of love, we are being generous with our opinion. We are acknowledging or assuming the best about that person. When we are making fear-based judgements, we are assuming the worst about that person based on our own inner dialogue, past experiences and insecurities. That is the interesting truth about judgment – it usually stems from our own insecurities. If we look at where our judgments come from, we will find that the roots are usually attached to something unhealed within ourselves.

Writing this portion of the chapter really put my own judgmental tendencies on display. In preparation for writing this chapter, I began to intentionally notice my own moments of judgment. I was amazed at how often and how quickly my mind unconsciously went into judgment; it was an automatic response on most days. I noticed that my inner hater is most often in the building when I get overwhelmed or haven't been consistent with my routines or self-care practices. It also comes up when I am feeling insecure about how I look or when I feel threatened in some way. Pretty much anytime that I am not feeling in alignment with my highest self, I find myself leading with judgment instead of acceptance.

I also noticed judgment flowing more easily from me when I was around people who I have known for a long time – especially if I had a history of gossiping with them. It's almost like I sometimes regress all the way back to when I was twenty-something, and I hear myself saying "GIRL! Guess what…?" Next thing I know I'm deep in a story I have absolutely NO business telling. That shit wasn't cute in high school, so it *definitely* isn't cute in adulthood! Even when we are a bit more evolved and self-aware, we can slip up. When we get together with old friends or family who we have a tendency to gossip with, the behavior can be automatic if we are not mindful.

It is, in its own corrosive way, a form of bonding between friends sometimes. It is also highly addictive. Studies show that gossiping can even raise our oxytocin levels. That little boost we get when we are "connecting" with friends through gossiping may feel good in the moment, but when you start to look at these seemingly harmless conversations about others, you will quickly see that they are indeed affecting you and your relationships. And to keep it extra real - if your friends are so quick to tell you about someone else's business, who's to say they aren't also telling people about your business, too? When we choose to gossip about others, our own credibility comes into question.

I invite you to pause and check in the next time you find yourself judging someone else. Allow yourself to unpack why you feel the need to make a judgmental comment or think a negative thought about someone else. Were you just in a bad mood? Or is it deeper? Is there something about them that triggers something within you? Or were you worried that you were being judged? What are the situations where you find yourself being more judgmental?

When you begin to fully look at the deeper reasons why you are judging others, you can begin to make that investigative view of yourself a practice. The more you can become aware of your triggers and insecurities, the less you will unconsciously judge others.

The other side of judgment is our fear of what others think about us - which is crazy - because if we are judging others, it's only logical to assume that it's being reciprocated. It's almost like we are using judgment or snarky comments as a shield to hide our own imperfections behind. Incredibly counterintuitive, but super common. At the end of the day, I think we all just want to be liked and we each (on some level) worry about how we are being perceived by others.

Journal Prompts

When do your inner critics most often show up? Do you see a pattern, if so, what usually triggers negative self-talk for you?

When you feel that inner critical voice objecting the next time, what will you commit to doing in order to stay true to yourself and your growth?

What are the situations where you find yourself being more judgmental?

How do you feel when you judge others for their mistakes or shortcomings?

CHAPTER FIVE:

You Are Worthy AF

"Everything that happens to you reflects what you believe about yourself. We cannot outperform our level of self-esteem. We cannot draw to ourselves more than we think we are worth." — Iyanla Vanzant

You are worthy – you began that way, and you will end that way. This is a universal truth. You are so incredibly worthy of feeling happy, supported, and unconditionally loved. You are worthy of living a life that you feel good about and comfortable in.

You, my friend, are worthy as fuck.

When I teach my weekly yoga classes, I end each session by reminding students of their worth. I tell them

speak align with the actions they take. This is what unwavering trust is built upon.

Now, back to you – how often are you doing the things you tell yourself you are going to do? If you are anything like I was a few years ago, you've failed yourself more times than you care to admit. How many New Year's Resolutions have been long forgotten by February 5th? How many *I'll start Monday* promises have come and gone and then Tuesday you feel like a flake because, once again you didn't do what you said you were going to do.

Firstly, know that you are not alone. These are common themes in most people's lives. The thing to be aware of while rebuilding trust in ourselves is that it's cumulative. The other side of this truth is that consistently *not* doing the things that we say we are going to do affects us negatively over time. Like everything else in life, this must become a practice; this is something we will have to consciously nurture until it becomes habitual.

The more positive momentum we build, the more we see ourselves following through on the things that matter most to us. The more momentum we build, the easier it becomes to do challenging things and the more confident we will feel in ourselves.

Flaws and All: Self-Acceptance

Another facet of our confidence comes from how we perceive ourselves physically. Feeling that we are somehow lacking physically or negatively focusing on our physical imperfections can also lead to feelings of unworthiness.

I was always someone who felt self-conscious physically; I was taller than most of the other girls in school and very skinny. Then, as a woman, there were new things to feel self-conscious about, from pregnancy stretch marks to c-section scars. Over the past several years, due to the severe digestive problems I experienced in 2014, old insecurities about my weight arose. I still get remarks like *why are you so skinny?* and *you should eat more!* because of my inability to keep weight on like I used to. Those kinds of remarks hit differently when the culprit is out of your control.

I still remember the tight feeling in my chest and how my stomach dropped when the emergency room doctor looked at me worriedly and said, "If we leave things how they are, you will not make it past tomorrow evening." I asked him what needed to happen for me to get better and once he answered, I immediately wished I hadn't asked.

"Well," he said after a long pause, "You're going to need to have a colostomy bag placed so we can remove the infection and let your colon heal for a few months."

Just seven days earlier, I was healthy, working full time and taking care of my two young sons. Then, out of nowhere, I started experiencing severe stomach pain and cramping – so intense that I rushed from my job to the emergency room. They did some scans and told me I had a small infection in my colon but that it would go away in a week or so. They put me on a clear liquid diet, gave me some pain meds, and sent me home. Three days later, I was back in the ER due to even worse stomach pain; this time it was so bad that I could barely walk or even stand up straight.

When the ER doctor explained what a colostomy bag was, I was shook. I didn't have much time to ponder this unexpected life change, which in hindsight, was a blessing. I remember waking up from surgery feeling groggy, then, remembering everything the doctor had explained. I lifted the blanket, saw the new accessory, and turned over to sob into my pillow.

Oh, how I cried.... I mean like snotty nosed, shoulders shuddering, leave your face swollen and red for hours, ugly cried. Imagine being 30 years old and having a colostomy bag placed. For those of you who don't know what a colostomy is, let me explain: one of the disconnected ends of my intestine was now protruding through the incision the surgeon had made in my stomach - my intestine was now *outside* my body. This little bright red thing, officially called a stoma, was where (wait for it) I would be pooping for the next several months. I was shitting into a bag that was like two inches away from my belly button.

I'll let that soak in – and my apologies for the visual... I just need you to understand the severity of this moment in time.

Once I went home and realized I would have to leave my house with this thing, I decided to temporarily stop the pity party to do some research. How did I hide this monstrosity?? What did other people do? Do other people my age even have this? After extensive research, I found out that people my age and even younger live with ostomies – some even have them for life. I felt extremely grateful that mine was temporary. As I began to research the health condition I had been afflicted with and how terribly it could've played out had I refused the poo-bag, I became increasingly grateful for my new appendage because it allowed me to live.

Although I had the bag for seven long months and it was a pretty shitty situation (pun intended), once I was able to positively reframe it, I was able to accept it more easily. As worried as I was about how I looked at that time, the real insecurities arose once I had the colostomy reversed. I was left with a belly full of strange scars. My belly button was permanently changed – adding to the strangeness that two pregnancies had created.

These insecurities really became apparent the following summer. As my social media feed began to get flooded with images of what a woman's body *should* look like, I was constantly reminded that my body didn't look like that anymore – and never would. Sure, I was slim, but now I have huge scars across my stomach. As I scrolled through countless flawless tummies, my feelings of unworthiness, shame and self-consciousness grew.

I know I am not alone in these feelings. Maybe you didn't have some crazy surgery that left your body permanently changed, but physical insecurities are very common and most of us have that THING that we struggle to accept. We all get caught in that comparison trap at some point in our adult lives, especially in this age of social media and filters.

Some things you can change by changing your habits and consistent work. But there are some that will become your new normal. I invite you to take extreme ownership of what you can change and make a commitment to yourself and how you want to feel. I will leave you with one of the things I discovered at a Narcotics Anonymous meeting many years ago, the Serenity Prayer:

God, grant me the serenity to accept the things I cannot change, the courage to change the things I can, and the wisdom to know the difference.

Identify what you can change and make an honest effort to change those things. If there are physical imperfections that you cannot change, practice a loving

69

perspective of acceptance. Allow your scars to be a reminder that you survived.

Treat Yo' Self: Self-Care

Self-care ties into the concept of worthiness nicely because it is something actionable that we can do to show ourselves how much we are worth. Making the decision to check in with yourself to discover what you need to feel safe and healthy is a powerful act of self-love. Self-care is also such a hot topic right now on social media – but how many of us are really practicing it? And are you even sure what qualifies as self-care? Here are a few of the responses I got from the participants of the 2019 Self Survey I did regarding their self-care practice:

I have a self-care day by myself at the beach or taking a long drive.

I practice self-care by being ok cutting out people and things that aren't good for me; people with negative energy and

outlook on life or friendships that were very one-sided.

For me, it's rest- making sure I get a good night's sleep or take naps if I need to.

I think it is so empowering to practice self-care because it is such a clear way of showing yourself how much you believe you are worth. It is also just the best way to create positive momentum in your life which enhances how you feel.

Be mindful of becoming a reactionary self-care practitioner: this is someone who waits until shit hits the fan or burn-out kicks in to start taking good care of themselves. When we operate from this place, we are forever playing a game of catch-up to calm down. It is so much more difficult to think clearly or make good choices while we are suffering. This concept makes me think of one of my favorite nurses from when I was hospitalized in 2014 - she would tell me to be sure and take my pain medicine right before it was due so I could "stay on top of the pain." I remember waiting too long a few times and it felt like it took hours for my pain to subside after taking the prescribed dose. Once we are already in the throes of pain or experiencing discomfort in our lives, it takes a lot longer for the medicine – in this case, self-care - to kick in.

Although I got some great feedback from people who actively practice self-care, there was another common theme that I found throughout the answers. A lot of people were falling into the *should* trap:

> *"I don't practice self-care, but I know I* ***should****"*
>
> *"I try to do it daily; I know I* ***should****, but I just don't have time."*
>
> *"I only do this, but I know I* ***should*** *be doing more"*

Ah, the notorious *should*. You have to be careful with that word because it can be incredibly shame inducing. When we are should-ing all over ourselves, we make a big mess of our self-belief. We often make ourselves wrong for not doing this thing we feel (or that we think other people feel) we *"should"* be doing. In order to nurture a healthy new routine or way of living, we need to move self-care from the *should* column to the *I want to because* column.

For starters, we must want to incorporate self-care because we want to take better care of ourselves, not because some chic on the internet said we *should*. I started practicing self-care for very specific reasons. I knew I wanted to feel better more of the time and be more productive, so I had to take a hard look at my self-care practice at the time (which was essentially nonexistent) I had the realization that if I wanted to get where I wanted to go, personally and professionally, I needed to get really clear on what filled my soul and cup back up.

And that's kind of the whole point, right? Filling our cup so we can operate at our highest capacity and with more ease. I remember watching an interview with Oprah Winfrey and she gave this great analogy that totally shifted how I viewed my life and the way I showed up for others. You know how you have a cup of tea on a saucer, right? Well, what she was saying was that our own cup must be full; so full that it is overflowing into our saucer and we serve from our saucer. This way, our cup remains full so that we can continue to serve but without experiencing burn-out which leads to resentment and low productivity. The best way to serve others is from our overflow because when our cup runneth over, we remain full.

Journal Prompts*:*

How would you show up differently in your life if you were more confident in yourself?

What situations or relationships have you experienced in the past that made you feel unworthy or not enough? What about those situations that made you feel that way?

What are the things about yourself that make you feel insecure?

If you were talking to yourself about this insecurity like you were talking to a friend, what would you say?

Write out the reasons why you want to incorporate a self-care routine. How will this enhance your life?

Write down at least three things that you can incorporate into your self-care practice.

CHAPTER SIX:

Tapping into Trauma

"Out of the suffering have emerged the strongest souls; the most massive characters are seared with scars." - Kahil Gibran.

So, why do so many of us struggle with the concept of self-worth? Why don't more of us truly believe in ourselves? And how do we cultivate feelings of worthiness so that we *can* raise our self-esteem?

There are many factors that contribute to low self-esteem. In my research for this book, I discovered an article by a psychiatrist in Oxford, England that confirmed my beliefs about where my own issues with self-worth stemmed from:

"Low self-esteem can be deeply rooted, with origins in traumatic childhood experiences such as prolonged separation from parent figures, neglect, or emotional, physical, or sexual abuse. In later life, self-esteem can be undermined by ill health, negative life events such as losing a job or getting divorced, deficient or frustrating relationships, and a general sense of lack of control. This sense of lack of control may be especially marked in victims of emotional, physical, or sexual abuse." (Neel Burton M.D. 2017)

Unprocessed trauma is one of the main reasons so many of us struggle with feelings of unworthiness. It is being openly discussed in more and more places, but what is not often mentioned is that we *all* have some level of trauma.

Trauma doesn't have to be a huge, life altering event like physical abuse or watching your home burn down. Trauma can stem from smaller instances too (i.e., financial worries or your parents getting divorced when you're a kid.) We have all walked through something that altered our view of the world and ourselves. How situations affect us will vary and is usually based on our past experiences, expectations, and beliefs. We then let these past experiences dictate our lives—usually unconsciously. Because we are not always taught how to properly experience our emotions as children, we can go years unconsciously playing out our unprocessed trauma in relationships without understanding why we continue to repeat unhealthy patterns.

I did this for many years.

Cultivating self-awareness through practices like meditation, journaling and yoga will allow you to create a safe space to explore why you do the things you do. They can help you identify where you are rough-around-the-edges emotionally so you can pinpoint what triggers those seemingly "too big" reactions. Our reactions help us identify our triggers so that we can become more aware of what situations bring up certain emotions or patterns of behavior and thought. Once we begin to understand ourselves better, we can show up more consciously in our lives. We will be kinder to ourselves and others because understanding self also breeds empathy. We are usually harder on others because we are so hard on ourselves internally.

Is it easy to look at past experiences that were hard, scary, or traumatic?

Of course not.

This is why you chose not to look at them to begin with. By being brave enough to look at our past trauma we can understand ourselves better. Digging deep and sorting through the rubble of past experiences is where the answers lie. The only way through something is exactly that—*through*. You cannot side-step around your shit if you truly want to heal. But you don't have to walk through this process alone. There are therapists, teachers and coaches who can be valuable resources, as well as tools and processes you can use to build your arsenal of self-healing.

Journaling is one of my favorite ways to work with my feelings. It provides a healthy form of release, but it also creates the space for self-reflection. Although it is important to release our emotions (more on this in the next chapter), it is equally as important to gain some understanding of what triggered that emotional response. My whole world changed when I had the language and context to identify what I was experiencing emotionally – for so many years I was told I was crazy or overly emotional because I would have these huge reactions that didn't quite fit the situations at hand. Now I know that when I feel a big emotion that doesn't fit what's happening in real time, I know that a deeper wound has been activated and that is when I know I need to pause and identify why I am feeling this.

Now, I don't always get it right (Lord knows....!) but the more I practice this pause and reflect technique, the less embarrassing freak-out moments I have. It can be difficult when our trauma is triggered by the words or actions of someone else, because when you are right up close to someone else, it's hard not to react automatically – especially when we are triggered. The best thing to do is walk away or call them back so you can go through your process of self-soothing and calming down.

I am going to share the journaling practice that I use when I am feeling triggered and need to pinpoint the source:

Part 1. The first part is releasing everything that is in your mind onto a piece of paper. A client of mine calls it her "brain dump". Do not worry about spelling, sentence structure, or grammar. Remember, no one is reading this so let it all the way out, and without judgment. Please take at least 10-15 minutes on this.

Once you feel like you've written all that you can, we can go to part 2.

Part 2: Identify the Trigger: Review what you wrote in the free write and identify the trigger. Ask yourself questions like *what was said or done that made you feel like this? When have you felt like this in the past – if so, what was that situation? Can you find a common denominator or thread of the recent times when you felt this trigger arise?* Writing out your answers to questions like these can assist in the brainstorming process.

Part 3: Self Soothe + Choosing Change: Now that you've released and reviewed, think about some healthy ways to begin to feel better. And write them out on your same journaling page. Ask yourself questions like *what can I do right now to feel better? What could I do next time I feel these bigger emotions arising?*

With practice you will have to write it out less and less as you realize your reactions are stabilizing. Also, don't expect yourself to get it perfect every time. Practice doing things differently on purpose so you can make changes and feel better in your relationships. Practice being patient and compassionate with yourself – wading through trauma is hard and confronting. If you don't get it right, it doesn't mean you've failed – it means you're human.

Suggested Mantras:

I embrace and explore my trauma with compassion so that I can release it.

I am resilient, strong, and supported. I am worthy of healing.

I am not my trauma; I am who I choose to become.

CHAPTER SEVEN:

All the Feels

"Feelings are really your GPS system for life. When you're supposed to do something, or not supposed to do something, your emotional guidance system lets you know." —Oprah Winfrey

Ah, emotions. Let's talk about all the feels, shall we?

As a woman, I know that expressing strong emotion is sometimes referred to as "being crazy", dramatic or overly emotional. Men are often taught that crying or showing emotion is a sign of weakness or "not manly." But who decided this bullshit? And why should we still have to abide by some outdated and narrow-minded ideas about how to feel our feelings? We don't have to. We get to choose how we process and express our emotions. As with most things that we have been conditioned to believe, it doesn't seem like we have a choice in the matter, but we do.

Our emotions can be useful indicators of where we are internally. When we feel a particular emotion arise, it is usually a clue to something deeper that is brewing. Emotions are meant to be expressed and released - but we must practice doing this in an ethical way. When we can learn to understand our emotions instead of stuffing, numbing, or projecting them, we can begin to cultivate a sense of unity and intelligence around them.

I did not always feel safe and synergy with the emotions that came up within me. I used to think that acknowledging and expressing my emotions was something that should never be allowed. I was raised in a home where if I cried, I was told to stop and that I was crying for attention or sympathy. I remember silently sobbing, shoulders shuddering uncontrollably into many pillows as a child. Later in life, I had boyfriends who told me similar things, so I decided that crying was not serving me. When we are told the same thing by multiple people, it seemingly validates the statement and we begin to believe it. This created the belief that expressing my emotions would always be misunderstood by others, so I needed to keep them hidden.

Looking back, no wonder why I felt so comforted by drugs; if my emotions were numb, there would be no tears. The ability to completely numb my emotions by getting high was a temporary respite from the big feelings that flowed through me all the time. But, when I stopped using drugs, I realized very quickly that I had a ton of huge emotions that I had absolutely no context for. I hadn't been given any healthy tools to face them with, so I often felt overwhelmed with emotions like anger, shame, and anxiety.

The tools that I've cultivated over the years to help me form a healthier relationship with my emotions are outlined in this chapter. With practice, you will discover a tiny space between feeling the emotions arise and getting lost in them. Over time, you'll be able to utilize your emotions in conjunction with your intuition to help guide you to the next right step. Allowing yourself to sit with and feel your emotions is the first step.

Allow Yourself to Feel It

Five years ago, if I would have flipped through a self-help book and seen a section in one of the chapters called *Allow Yourself to Feel It*, I would've gingerly placed the book back on the shelf, rolled my eyes and left in search of a romance book with some juicy sex scenes in it. Although I was beginning to become sort of intrigued by the idea of taking more ownership of my life, that just would have been taking things entirely too far.

It wasn't until my yoga teacher training in 2016 that I finally learned to sit with my big emotions. I walked in nervous about getting the poses wrong since I had never done yoga in front of another human being, but little did I know that Yoga goes so much deeper than shapes on a mat.

It was the first time I was in the presence of individuals who were encouraging me to observe my feelings and to honor them. When we would do our breath work (in yoga we call in pranayama) during classes, the teacher would ask us to witness our thoughts and then our emotions. She would guide us to notice how the emotion felt in our bodies, which I had never even considered in my thirty-two years of existence.

I'm not going to lie, at first, I was very apprehensive and resistant towards all the acknowledging emotions business.

What if I start crying and can't stop? What if they judge me? Will I want to start getting high again if I face all these deep emotions inside me? Can I even be a yoga teacher if I have so many dark emotions? These were the thoughts that raced through my mind during those first few days of teacher training. When I would get super emotional and cry in front of my fellow trainees, I remember wondering to myself *am I ok, is this normal??* I had suppressed so much for so long, and because of the messaging I received during childhood and within romantic relationships, my reaction to strong emotion was *that something was wrong with me.*

What I realized when I did allow myself to explore my emotions while I sat there breathing on my mat, was that I felt so much freedom through allowing myself to sit with my emotions. I felt that because I had finally observed my emotions, they could no longer control me. I was able to have compassion for them instead of disdain towards them . That is how I know you must allow yourself to feel your emotions if you want to discover that sense of freedom and ease within yourself.

I know from experience how foreign and sometimes unsafe leaning into our emotions can seem initially. But you have to allow the emotion to come up so you can look at it and experience it. If that means cry, then cry. Try to look at tears as a release. As I tell my students who've gotten a little teary eyed in a yoga class, we would not have the ability to cry if this wasn't a necessary function of release.

Yoga tends to show us parts of ourselves that we otherwise resist. It is one of my favorite ways to drop in and get clear on what's going on internally. How I show up in a difficult pose is usually how I show up in difficult times in life. After I practice yoga, I am more aware of my thoughts and breathing so I can notice when emotions arise much faster and I can regulate with intelligence instead of blindly projecting my emotions onto others or spiraling unconsciously into a loop of negative thoughts and emotions.

Meditation is also a great way to begin the process of exploring the emotions that regularly come up within you. The next time you sit down to meditate, keep some conscious awareness on the body; notice how your body reacts when certain thoughts come up. Our body can show us how we are feeling emotionally if we tune into it on a regular basis. For example, when I am stressed, my breath gets short and my shoulders creep up towards my ears. My jaw clenches and my forehead wrinkles between my eyebrows. Through meditation I can practice relaxing those areas while simultaneously setting myself up for success by deepening my breathing. The deeper you breathe, the more you will calm the body and mind – meditation literally helps you regulate your nervous system and takes you from fight or flight to insight.

Also, be mindful not to project your pain onto others; do not blame or hurt anyone in a fit of strong emotion. But do create a safe space for release. This can be therapy or a trusted friend. This can be time alone or journaling all the cuss words and mean comments in order to release and move past them. Learn to lean in so when big feelings inevitably arise, you know how to work with them instead of using valuable energy to resist them. We cannot always control what happens around us, but it is ultimately our responsibility to do the work of processing our emotions in a healthy way. It's a practice and you won't always get it right, so be easy on yourself when you are starting out. As with everything else in life, the more you do it, the easier it becomes.

Give Yourself a Time Limit

Did you know that most emotions only last about 90 seconds? What keeps us locked into that feeling, though, is the story we create and the thoughts we allow to go on and on in our minds. Think back to the last time you felt super emotional. How long did you stay in that space before you started really marinating in negative thoughts? Often, we will feel an emotion and be upset about it for a time, but what brings that lingering dark cloud is when we start getting all up in our heads about the feeling or situation. We create an entire story around the situation and continue to replay the story in our minds, fueling the flame of negativity. That is when we can spiral down a darker hole and sometimes even into feelings of depression.

This is where we can incorporate a time limit for the time spent in the dark place. As we just discussed, you have to allow yourself to feel the emotion in order to release it. One of the main differences between feeling the emotion and marinating in it is the amount of time and energy spent in that space. Was I always good at navigating my emotions in this way?

Absolutely not.

Back in the day, I would be petty as hell and start talking about it for far too long, which just kept it present in my energy. But who does that serve? No one. The other person usually doesn't even know that you are mad, so you are just keeping yourself from joy.

Depending on the situation, I will give myself anywhere from ten minutes to a couple of hours to be mad about something. If it is something from work, an hour is the most I will spend on it. I feel anger or hurt and then I do the work to reframe it. I think about the situation objectively and try to put myself in the other person's shoes. I ask myself how this negative emotion serves me. I ask myself if I am overreacting. And I ask myself if this situation truly affects my life in a major way moving forward; usually the answer is no. The key is to avoid letting the thoughts that follow the emotions take you into negative obsessing for days at a time.

There are still days when I am tired or not feeling my best that I find myself lost in feelings of blame, judgment or self-pity. The goal is to create more self-awareness and healthy discipline around our emotions. The more we practice checking in when we are in the heat of our negative emotions, the less we will get caught aimlessly spiraling down Negative Nancy Lane.

For bigger situations, give yourself more time. When we are talking about something like grief, we must take it in the waves that it comes in. My adoptive mother passed away when I was pregnant with my second son in 2012, and it was incredibly difficult to navigate. When you're pregnant, you are already incredibly emotional at times, so I was extremely raw during this time. I felt so much emotion because I was five months pregnant and because our relationship had been strained and almost nonexistent in the years leading up to her death.

There will be seasons in your life when the emotions will be big and they will feel unmanageable. Make sure you continue to breathe and take good, conscious care of yourself. You don't have to try and be the strong one during times of grief. Allow yourself to acknowledge your big feelings and especially during these times, reach out for support and be easy on yourself. I know from experience that time, accompanied by conscious effort can truly heal all if you allow it to.

Allow Others to Hold Space for You

I am also a huge advocate for therapy. The misconception about therapy is that something has to be "wrong" or we need to be in some sort of major emotional crisis. This could not be further from the truth. I was joking with a friend recently when we were discussing her desire to start therapy again, that we take better care of our cars than we do of our own emotional wellbeing! We take our cars in for oil changes and tire rotations, but when it comes to our emotions, we sort of wing it and hope for the best only seeking professional help when shit hits the fan. When we shift from reactive to proactive, we hold the power and we become the drivers of our emotional vehicles.

The other key is having friends and/or mentors that you can turn to when you need to just work through emotions verbally. Cultivate friendships that nurture you and allow you space to process how you're feeling. Be aware of when venting becomes complaining – there is a major difference. Venting should have an end point and there must be some intention behind it (i.e. get it out so you can let it go!). If you find yourself just rehashing the same situation repeatedly with no real end goal, then you have ventured into complaining and this is not conducive to finding solutions or healthy release.

Journal Prompts

Think about an experience that made you feel painful emotions. What thoughts did you have about this experience? Did the thoughts prolong or ease the emotion?

What negative emotions surface most often around it (like anxiety, shame, or sadness)?

When you feel negative emotions arising next time, what can you do to greet them that is new and healthy?

When you practice sitting with emotions, what comes up for you? (this can be physical sensations and/or thoughts.)

CHAPTER EIGHT:

Forgiveness + Letting Go

"Forgiveness is the fragrance that the violet sheds on the heel that has crushed it." — *Mark Twain*

My greatest lesson in forgiveness came from infidelity. It is interesting how so many of our greatest learning opportunities are hidden within some truly painful experiences.

I was happy and finally in a relationship where I felt loved and was being treated like a queen. Sure, there were some red flags, which at the time, I just assumed all relationships had some red flags. But he cooked and cleaned and did all the things my ex didn't, so it was good, right?

Wrong.

I saw the signs: sneaky behavior with his cell phone, lots of female friends who were extremely attractive and around my age, calling me insecure or crazy when I asked any questions about these friendships and late-night texts and phone calls. But I was so ready for a partnership and he had so many qualities the last ones didn't, that I chose to overlook those things from the beginning, assuming (well, desperately hoping) things would change and he would come to his senses and realize he was messing up something good.

That's the thing about allowing behaviors that you know are not ok with to continue unchecked – it becomes almost impossible to demand change later on because you've allowed it initially.

I remember about a year in when things were getting really bad, I was no longer even speaking up about all the things I saw, because there were so many, that I felt I had to be strategic about what I bought up in fear that I would seem overbearing or be called crazy and insecure.

I had made the mistake of being very vulnerable with him about my abandonment stuff which manifested as trust issues from my parents dying at a young age, so now when I would ask him where he had gone or who was calling at 2am on a Saturday night, he would lash out and tell me how crazy I was and to "not take your baggage out on me!"

I would turn to my journal and get everything out because if I didn't, I would have quite literally lost my mind. After a while I stopped asking. I became more and more withdrawn and unhappy. My feelings of unworthiness heightened, and I began to wonder what I was doing wrong. *I know I'm a good woman,* I would think bleakly to myself, *why would he want someone else?*

One morning, after a particularly bad night, I woke up early but pretended to be asleep until he left for work at 6:30am. After he left, I broke down crying into my pillow. Here I was in this beautiful house, in these expensive sheets and I was miserable; my heart was breaking. I had been told I was crazy so many times that I began to wonder if maybe he was right. Maybe I was making this all up and letting my own issues get the best of me.

I decided to get up instead of lying there wallowing in my own desperate confusion. It was winter, so I headed to our walk-in closet to grab one of my hoodies. When I realized mine were all dirty I went to his side of the closet to grab one of his. As I pulled the smallest one I could find from underneath all the others, three condoms fell off the shelf also. I stood there for a moment staring down at the three Trojans.

We used condoms the very first time we had sex and never after. I also had a hysterectomy two years prior, so there were no fears of pregnancy either. I stood there for what felt like an eternity before I realized I was violently shaking. Then I had a thought, *I have proof!* There was no way he could talk his way out of this now.

Looking back, I can see how toxic this all was, but while I was in it, it felt so normal; its amazing the things we can normalize before we know what we deserve.

When I confronted him about it, I was almost giddy – I had waited months to have something tangible to bring him so he would finally admit to his shady behavior. He immediately got defensive and insisted that the condoms had been there since before we met. He then went into his same speech about me being crazy and jealous, but this time I didn't back down.

"Do you know how many times I have cleaned that fucking closet?!" I yelled furiously. Thirteen months of pent-up fury escaped my lips like fire. He proceeded to match my increasing volume until I finally backed down, only because I did not want my children to hear us. I submitted, again, even though I intuitively knew the truth. His argument, as always, placed doubt on my own internal knowing. He left and I was, yet again, on the floor crying uncontrollably.

As I looked at the carpet fibers that I knew so well, I prayed for the first time in months. *Please God, show me what I am not seeing,* I repeated that prayer silently and fervently in my mind. Two weeks later, I discovered the hotel receipts and text messages from when I was at work and the whole thing finally (and quite violently) unraveled.

Although he denied anything happening there, I had enough proof. It turned out to be the same woman who had been introduced to me as his "play sister" that I had felt uneasy about from the beginning of our relationship. This was crushing for me emotionally. I could not fathom how someone could so intricately play into someone's trauma and past pain and not feel bad about it. It was one of the lowest moments of my adult life.

That first year after I left him, I had moved out, but I had not moved on. I held onto so much anger and hurt; I kept replaying the scenario in my mind and retelling it to friends. I realize now this kept me locked in a space of hurt and anger and that was keeping me from peace, from forgiveness. In my mind, he didn't deserve forgiveness for intentionally hurting me the way he did. It was not until I had the understanding of why I should forgive that I was able to move forward and find meaning and peace in the situation.

When we forgive others, it helps us with our healing process. Depending on the experiences in your life, you may question the validity of that statement; there are some hurts that feel unforgivable – trust me, *I know*. But remember, forgiveness isn't about condoning their behavior in any way, it is about letting go of toxic, negative emotions so they don't poison our minds and bodies and hearts. By letting go of the hate and hurt we are holding onto, we clear space for ease and peace and love. The other byproduct of forgiveness is compassion, and when we can access compassion for others, we are more likely to be compassionate toward ourselves.

Choose to Forgive Yourself, Too

The other huge piece I want to tap into is the idea of forgiving yourself. Often, when we look back on situations, we see where we could have made better or different choices; we get caught in a shame cycle as we blame ourselves for not seeing that particular outcome or situation coming.

After that relationship ended, I realized I didn't trust myself. I would silently berate myself for not speaking up sooner or not getting involved when the red flags were so apparent. It was like I needed someone to blame for this pain I was so immersed in and the only ones I could blame were he and I so that's what I did for that first several months on my own again.

Desperate for peace, I began meditating. After a week of daily practice, I began to notice the patterns of thought that kept bringing me back to the feelings of blame and self-pity. I noticed that I would think a certain thought or have a conversation and that would trigger the cycle of emotional pain and fragility. Once I knew the things that triggered the negative emotions, I consciously thought a new thought and stopped having those kinds of conversations.

You see this is why self-awareness is so valuable – when we are aware of our triggers and patterns, we can make changes that help us feel better. Once I had emotional distance, I was able to separate myself from his choices. Yes, I could've done things differently, but I didn't. And that is ok. The important thing about forgiving ourselves is that we give ourselves some grace. When we know better, we do better and beating ourselves up about not knowing better is, well, just plain crazy.

Journal Prompts

Who in my life do I need to forgive?

How would forgiving this person or situation change my life and how I feel?

What are some things I need to forgive myself for and why?

What comes up emotionally when I try to access forgiveness?

CHAPTER NINE:

F*ck Fear + Playing Small

"There is only one thing that makes a dream impossible to achieve: the fear of failure." —Paulo Coelho, The Alchemist

One of my greatest fears is getting to the end of my life and looking back with regret. I remember hearing someone say that on a podcast a couple of years ago and it hit me hard. It made me think about my life through the lens of mortality. I lost my parents incredibly young; well, I have lost a lot of people who were close to me. While obviously sad to have seen so much death early on in life, it has its positive side effects. It has gifted me a lens of mortality motivation.

Another reason why I wanted to write this chapter was because of what I learned through completing my Yoga teacher training – it was such an *ah-ha!* moment for me.

When I walked into The Pad Yoga studio in San Francisco on September 2016, I was already overwhelmed.

Shit, I was overwhelmed before I even got in the car an hour prior to driving over there. I was thirty-two and had never been inside of a yoga studio before. Of course, I had practiced Yoga some, but all my experience was at home, alone following a YouTube video—I had never actually done Yoga in front of another human being before. Outside of warrior two, downward dog and maybe child's pose, I didn't even know the names of the poses let alone if I was doing them correctly!

It seems a little crazy to think about, but also cosmic – I didn't consciously know then that this practice and the wisdom it possessed would change my life forever, but on some level I must've known because I did this seemingly crazy thing.

Flustered from attempting to find parking in Downtown San Francisco at 4:00pm on a Friday (I lived an hour away in what seemed like "the country" in comparison), I entered the studio and asked the woman at the front desk where to go. She was blonde and kind and welcoming; she cheerfully asked me to remove my shoes and head into the main room where the studio was. Palms still sweating from my death grip on the steering wheel, I walked into the doorway and looked around.

There were about thirty women in there chatting with one another. They were all white and they all looked like…. well, what I imagined Yoga people to look like. My mouth went dry and I turned around abruptly to go back out the front door.

"Lindsey?" I heard from behind me.

Already halfway out the front door, I turned over my shoulder to see the woman at the desk looking a little confused.

"I'll be right back, I forgot something in my car," I blurted out, face burning with embarrassment and anxiety. She smiled and nodded, and I booked it up Union Street. I stopped about a block down and caught my breath. *What the fuck am I doing???* I thought to myself. I decided to call a good friend of mine to ask her what to do.

"Everyone is blonde and they have way nicer outfits and I don't think I can do this!" I whined, "One girl looked like sixteen! I think I should just wait until I have more experience—I've never even been to a Yoga class!"

"GIRL! You better take your ass back in there!" she said, "This is something you really wanted to do; besides, you drove all the way there. At least stay for the first day."

So, I went back. I scanned the room again and found a woman who had dark curly hair and a big smile. I smiled back and sat down next to her. We started chatting and soon realized we had more than just our curls in common. I started to feel more at ease and within the first two hours of that first day, I knew I was in the right place.

Sure, I messed up on many poses and there were moments where I felt super self-conscious, but I was there and I was doing it. Over time I learned the names of the poses and the names of all the name brand Yoga clothes the girls wore. By stepping way outside of my comfort zone, I stepped into a circle of sisterhood that I will have and cherish for life.

Imagine if I had gotten into my car and driven home that day. I wouldn't be a yoga teacher, I wouldn't be the woman I am today, and I definitely wouldn't be writing this particular book.

There was so much power in feeling that fear and then doing it anyway. Up until that point, I had repeated fear-based patterns, playing small out of fear of judgment or fear of failing in front of others. I worried what people would think of me if I stepped outside of who they perceived me to be.

How exhausting…

No wonder why I felt low-level anxiety and frustration for the first twelve years of my adult life! I was so consumed by other people's opinions and the fear that people wouldn't like me anymore if I changed, that I was suffocating my own soul. I was playing small in hopes that I wouldn't upset or alarm anyone. I walked around with so much resentment because I was people pleasing when in reality, and what I didn't realize at the time, was that the person to blame was myself. Regardless of why, I was choosing to show up in this way.

You see, although I was worried about what others thought and conformed to what I assumed (or what they told me) they expected of me, it was ultimately my choice to live within those restricting confines. The lens I was looking at life through was not an empowering one, it was keeping me from being my best self.

Think back to a time in your life where you really wanted to pursue something but didn't because of fear. Maybe you wanted to run a 5k or start a yoga practice but were worried you couldn't do it so you just didn't try. Did that desire go away? Probably not. Sure, you stopped talking about it, but I guarantee you did not stop thinking about it.

That's the thing about what we truly want for our lives – it never goes away. It may change and you may talk yourself out of the idea that you want that thing, but the desire if ignored or squandered will transmute into that low-level frustration and low sense of self-worth. We are meant for so much more than we usually set out to achieve. I honestly believe that God (or the universe, or spirit – whatever higher power you believe in) does not put a calling on our hearts in vain – if you can't stop thinking about it, it is meant for you.

My hope for you, for all of us, is that you choose right now to stop squandering the potential and silent dreams that reside within you. Only you know what that thing is that you want to be or do or have – please don't allow playing small out of fear rob you of what is meant for you.

Imposter Syndrome

Another thing that can come up, especially when we do break through the fear and do it anyway, are the feelings of "I don't belong." This is called imposter syndrome and I am oh-so-familiar with it. The best example of this that I can give you for imposter syndrome was the first two years after I stopped using drugs. Although I was no longer using it, I would still get major anxiety and felt like a "tweaker".

I remember when I got a job at my local community college and I was being trained by my new boss. I felt so surprised that they trusted me to do the job, hell, I was surprised they trusted me at all! Although I was doing all the right things and being an honest employee, I remember feeling almost guilty because I knew the life I was coming from and the people that I had been associating with. It was like even though I had removed myself physically from that life, the shadow of those experiences still hung over me like a dark cloud of shame.

Often when we embark on the journey of creating a new life for ourselves, which requires us to show up in completely new ways, it can feel false. Because it feels new and we do not know this new person yet, we feel like an imposter. This is normal and will pass.

There may also be people in your life that will not be accepting of this new you; because they have known you to be a certain way, you are stepping outside of that, and it may appear fake to them. Remember that you are not here to shrink yourself into anything you've outgrown in hopes of appeasing the next person – like I said earlier, if you choose to play small out of fear of what others may think about it, you can only blame yourself. This is your life, this is your journey. Keep going in the direction of your dreams even if no one around you understands. And if you find that the majority of the people in your world don't support or understand you, it is probably time to create a new sphere of friends.

Journal Prompts

What dreams or goals do you have for yourself?

In what areas of your life are you playing small? Why do you think that is?

What would your life look like if you felt the fear and still did what you wanted anyway?

What small, actionable steps could you take towards your goal each day or each week?

CHAPTER TEN

But First, Self-Love

self-love

noun

regard for one's own well-being and happiness

I never had an example of a healthy partnership growing up. The woman that raised me lived alone for the duration of my time there and there were never conversations about what it meant to be in a healthy relationship. Because my childhood was so sheltered and I couldn't even really watch television outside of kids' shows (if I was lucky) and the 7 'o' clock news, I didn't even have those examples to look to for some sort of context.

Now, adding in the abandonment and low self-worth issues that came from my mom doing drugs (which

I, at the tender age of 5, internalized as "mom chose drugs over me, therefore I am not important/worthy/loved") I entered my adult relationships with baggage and an unspeakable number of insecurities. Since I was seeking partners from a broken and wounded place, I was making poor choices and attracting men who also undervalued themselves or needed fixing.

Although as I got older, I did get a little wiser, it wasn't until I consciously stopped repeating the cycle of rushing into relationships for the wrong reasons. In 2017, I ended a relationship and realized that I was the common denominator in all my relationships. I also no longer trusted my judgment because my pattern of poor choices was now undeniable. Something had to change, and for the first time, I realized it was *me*.

Whew.

That is some hard shit to come to terms with – especially when it's so much easier to just point to the things the other person did wrong. It's justified and all your friends will agree with you because you're not wrong. In all the relationships I was in, there were obvious issues that were brought by the opposing party.

But that doesn't really serve us; it doesn't create the space for us to grow and make better choices moving forward.

You see, taking two years without a romantic relationship allowed me so much more than clarity around what I wanted in my next partner. It showed me the wounds that I had that led to me making the choices I had made. It wasn't about "them" at all. It was about first getting clear on what baggage I bring to relationships and after unpacking that, understanding what I deserve. It was about me, finally taking the time to get to know myself. The unexpected and sacred byproduct of unpacking my baggage, trauma and unhealthy patterns, was access to self-respect and a true understanding of self-love.

I had left my previous relationship heartbroken – I was a hot mess. I honestly didn't think I could trust someone again let alone try another relationship, so I decided I was done dating. My first, consistent meditation practice began at this time. Sometimes the external world feels overwhelming and meditation becomes a respite from all the triggers. Over time it even helped me dive deeper into my own choices and desires.

As time passed, I felt better, but I made the decision not to date. I didn't even have sex with anyone new that first year I was single. I knew I had to get clear on what I wanted and what my non-negotiables were. I had never done that before, and since I had no desire to date due to the events that occurred within my previous relationships, it was the perfect time to intentionally be alone.

As I began to unpack the relationships of my past, how they ended and my role in what went wrong, I realized my partners weren't solely to blame for the demise of our relationship. The fact that I had just begun to process some of my childhood trauma helped me dive deeper into how I felt and also created a safe space to explore and identify my triggers.

I got crystal clear on what I needed in a relationship – without worrying that I was asking too much. I was finally realizing my value as a woman. I really took stock of what I brought to the table. And although I do bring some not-so-great issues and baggage for many reasons, I also brought a huge amount of positive qualities.

In the spring of 2019, I started to feel like I might be ready to start dating again. After all, it had been a little over two years. I went on a couple dates and neither felt right so I wondered if maybe I maybe just wasn't ready yet. They both had great jobs and nice homes, but I never felt fully comfortable in their presence. The conversations felt surface and limited, and I didn't feel the kind of connection I desire from a romantic relationship. I realized very quickly that I wasn't going to find "The One" in my hometown. So, I decided to just put all my energy into teaching yoga and my writing. Once I figured out where I wanted to relocate to, then I could worry about that kind of stuff later.

But, per usual, life had different plans. I fell in love.

I wasn't planning on it, nor was I actively looking. He was delivered to my desk by one of my closest friends on campus; someone I had worked with for twelve years and also someone who had never brought a man to meet me.

"Hey Lindsey!" I heard a familiar voice say cheerfully behind me, and I quickly swiveled around in my desk chair, excited to see him. I saw my friend

117

standing there with another man whom I also immediately recognized. My friend introduced us, totally unaware that I knew this person he had brought to my desk.

"I know you!" I blurted out, and instantly began to blush at my way too eager statement. I remembered him from ten years prior when he was a student at the community college I worked at. We hadn't been friends or even had a conversation, but we'd had some of the same acquaintances at that time. Now he was all grown up, not that he wasn't then, but he was a grown man now and it showed – in a good way.

He and I exchanged pleasantries after my friend had walked over to a colleague's desk to get help with some paperwork. We chatted for a bit and before he left, he handed me his card.

After they left, I decided to email him saying how great it was to see him and that I was impressed with all the great things he was doing professionally for himself. He replied quickly and asked how we could stay connected, so we exchanged phone numbers. We had our first phone conversation a few days later, the first of many.

Since he lived and worked in New York, I didn't have expectations that this would be a viable relationship option. We would talk on the phone, usually for hours, about everything. I think because I didn't look at him as a partner prospect at the time, I was fully comfortable being myself. I realized within a month that there was a unique and undeniable connection between us. We were both incredibly busy – him coaching college football at a major university, and me working full time at the community college while also teaching Yoga and beginning to write this book, so the daily communication between us spoke volumes about how we felt about each other. We took the time and effortlessly to communicate and this allowed communication to become the foundation of our relationship.

Twenty-two flights, almost two years and an entire pandemic later, we still talk every single day. Our friendship became a committed, romantic relationship several months after we met. While the distance between us makes it difficult sometimes, it was also a blessing because it forced us to become friends first. Because communication was truly all we had for most of our relationship, it allowed us to create a bond based on friendship and understanding instead of my usual pattern of having sex, jumping right into a "relationship", and then realizing that I don't really even know (or like!) the person in front of me. The other huge part of why this worked – at least for me - was the years I had taken to intentionally be by myself and doing the work to look at all my shit.

It hasn't been all butterflies and rainbows though; aside from the arduousness of maintaining a long-distance relationship, the most difficult aspect of this relationship has been managing new and resurfacing trust issues—with myself and within the relationship. Relationships are like mirrors in that way, aren't they?

See, I thought that because I had done all that work and spent two years facing all my issues surrounding relationships, that I would totally crush it in my next relationship. And, while I am doing so much better than I ever have, triggers still arise based on my past experiences. The thing about healing and personal evolution is that it takes time and is not always linear. But that doesn't mean it isn't happening and that it doesn't serve us the do the work to heal old wounds. I mean, those are ultimately our two choices: to do the internal work and heal so we can become who we are meant to become or intentionally stay the same, which forces us to repeat the same patters to varying degrees with different people.

You may be wondering how this unexpected love story relates to self-development. Well, it's everything. Not him of course, but more about what I am learning about myself through this partnership. It was easy to feel healed when there was no one up close to trigger my old issues. But the true test is when we are in real time facing something that reminds us of our past.

We try to seek and find the perfect person but what most of us fail to realize is that we must first *become* the right person. We must also understand how we need to be loved. By taking the time to be alone for awhile while I learned more about myself and my choices, I unintentionally discovered the importance and true meaning of self-love.

Self-love is first a choice and then a practice; it requires conscious and consistent maintenance. I used to think that it was something I would arrive at and everything would feel different. I would see people post about self-love and the idea resonated, but I wasn't sure how to get there. As I began to research more and sit with myself to reflect, I realized that it wasn't a destination at all—it's a journey.

The journey to self-love will require extreme honesty and accountability. The journey to and understanding of self-love will be an ongoing unfolding of layers that you may not even know are there. You will arrive at a new level of self-acceptance and comfortability, only to be shown yet another layer that needs to be peeled back, examined, and either nurtured, or discarded.

Now that I have described this sort of painful and grueling process, let me give you the good news: Everything that you have read so far in this book has been pointing you here. All the practices and tools for reflection were meant to get you closer to yourself, and to the understanding of who you are. The final piece to truly embodying who you're meant to become is understanding self-love.

Have you ever heard someone say "you can't love someone else if you don't love yourself"? Well, it's partially true.

Partially.

You can, in fact, love someone else if you haven't fallen in love with who you are. The caveat here is that you cannot maintain truly healthy relationship dynamics when you are coming from a place of not loving who yourself.

Self-love is tricky and will sometimes feel elusive. Even when you feel love for who you are and all you've walked through, you will still have days that you just don't like yourself. This doesn't mean self-love has forsaken you. Think about your closest, most meaningful relationships; the people you would do just about anything for because you love them so much. Aren't there days that you also don't like those people? I have had conversations with fellow mothers who, in the heat of a hard moment with their kids, have exclaimed with exasperation, "I know this sounds terrible but I don't like my kid right now!"

What I am hoping you can understand here is that it's not even humanly possible to like another person every single day, so why should your feelings about yourself be held to an unrealistic standard?

Self-love requires us to show up for ourselves first. Just like when you are on an airplane and the flight attendant tells you to put your mask on first before anyone else, we must first make sure we are ok (mentally, emotionally and sometimes even physically) before we can help someone else in a meaningful way.

Haters will say this is toxic.

But I stand firmly on this belief, because I know from experience what the alternative looks and feels like. I lived over thirty years of my life not loving myself. At this point in the book, you are very familiar with the why of this so we won't rehash. I just need you to understand why my position is so strong on this. My relationships were terrible, I was not a great mother, and I always felt... unhappy. I was expecting other people to fill that void within and when they inevitably fell short, I would blame them and sink deeper into sadness. It wasn't until I looked inward and began this inner exploration that I realized the love I was seeking began in me. Sure, others could mirror it back to me, but I no longer desperately needed that to occur just to feel ok.

I am a better mother because I chose to begin taking care of my mental health and finding things that fulfilled me outside of motherhood. Of course, my kids fulfill me, but outside of being their mom, I am a woman.

It would be unfair and would feel strangling to them if I required them to be my only source of fulfillment and purpose. That is an unfair expectation to have of children, or anyone really. The beautiful byproduct of this is that my kids get to see, in real time, what it looks like to evolve and have tools to help you through hard times and emotions. They get to know what it looks like to reach for more in life and what healthy hard work can manifest. They have watched me wake up at 5am daily to write this book and record podcasts. I do this for myself because I want to feel fulfilled and have a deeper sense of purpose. I do it for them because I want them to reach for more and know that they too can do anything they want in their lives. I do most of my work before they get up so I am not taking quality time from them. Self-love isn't selfish and it will enhance your relations with others

Self-love isn't just about buying yourself stuff or repeating affirmations; it is about finding what lights you up and doing more of that. It is about listening in to what you need instead of solely looking outside of yourself for what needs tending to. It's about allowing yourself to feel your big, sometimes messy feelings and choosing to begin again the next day with earnest.

The bottom line is, if we do not consciously attempt to love ourselves regularly, we will begin to feel that low-grade frustration or sadness. We will not have the emotional bandwidth to be healthy partners or parents. Hell, we won't even know what healthy relationships feel like because we will be trying to pull everything we think we need from the other person and soon, that relationship will be suffocated.

No person can make you feel better about yourself; no one person can love you enough to make you feel whole…

My promise to you is this: if you've read this book and are doing the practices, you will begin to understand yourself more. As you make the necessary shifts in your life and mindset, you will create the space to truly explore who you are and all the amazing qualities you possess. Once we understand ourselves (our light and our wounds) we cultivate compassion, and with true compassion comes love.

Journal Prompts

What comes to mind when you think of self-love?

Have you ever taken inventory of your past relationships? If so, what did you learn/realize about yourself? If you haven't ever much reflection on your past relationships, why do you think that is?

What is one small change you could start tomorrow morning to check in with yourself and do something just for you?

What have you experienced in past relationships that creates issues in your current relationships? What hurts (or maybe guilt) are you acting out in your current or most recent relationships?

CONCLUSION

You Got This

Well, here we are. You made it to the end. First, congratulations.

I hope you are feeling empowered and excited about what's to come. I hope you believe in your heart that you can change your life. My hope is that you really take this opportunity to look at your life through a lens of love and compassion. I mean, haven't you judged yourself or complained enough about your life?

It's time to take what you've learned and put your money where your mouth is. It is time to go from just talking about what you "wanna do" or what you're "gonna do" and take actionable steps towards the life you wish to create.

Remember: healing and creating lasting change in your life is a process. These are tools and ideas that you can return to as life happens to reassess and make sure you and still move in the direction of your goals and dreams.

You must first get to know yourself through intentional self-awareness practices. Learn to sit with yourself so you can stop the cycle of numbing and running and hiding from your wounds as well as your truths.

You now also know the power of choice and importance of habits. You know how to ease the voice of the inner critic and tune into the voice that reminds you of your worth. I pray you never forget that you are worthy AF. If you take nothing else from this book, please know your innate worth as a human being.

We have walked through the exploration of trauma and big emotions and forgiveness. Whew! That is some big shit but you did it. But probably most importantly, you have a better understanding of self-love. As I said in the last chapter, self-love is the ultimate goal. We cannot arrive or even genuinely understand self-love into we heal.

My final hope for you is that you remember what you have learned within these pages about life and love and yourself. I hope you continue to fall down, feel it all, and get back up with renewed faith and confidence in yourself and your ability to be great. I pray that this book has been a beautifully raw reminder that you can do hard things.

So, go forth, and become. You got this!

Acknowledgments

I have fantasized about getting to this last page for my book where I could thank everyone who inspired me along the way; to officially shout out the ones who stuck with me as I ugly cried and doubted myself.

Thank you to my girls who kept me sane and acted as therapists and sisters and reminders of who I am and who I have been. Being rooted in such realness kept me from losing my easily distracted mind.

Thank you to my kids who cheered me on while also making sure I practiced what I preached. Thank you both for keeping me in check and on my toes.

Thank you to Diamond for living up to the meaning of your name and for reminding me of what I deserve in life and love.

Thank you to Joshua for showing me what true strength and "doing the work" looks like. Thank you for being a teacher and friend.

Thank you to my many friends and colleagues at SRJC. I grew up in Admissions and Records and on that campus. While my experience and journey to get there weren't the normal pathways, I am grateful for my "college experiences."

Shout out to LaKeela Smith for the beautiful cover photo.

About the Author

Lindsey Cacy is a mother, yoga teacher, and author. She believes that the first step to healing and feeling good is cultivating self-awareness – we cannot heal what we refuse to look at. The more we heal, the more we can access unconditional love. In her classes, she invites  students to go deep and to access their true emotions: get quiet, get to know yourself and start creating the life you genuinely want.

When she's not teaching yoga, Lindsey spends time with her two sons, writing and sharing vulnerably on her self-development podcast, Choose to Become.

To hear more from Lindsey, check out her podcast, Choose to Become, and her blog, www.lindseycacy.com/blog. Connect with her on social media – just search Lindsey Cacy on Facebook, Instagram, and Twitter.

CPSIA information can be obtained
at www.ICGtesting.com
Printed in the USA
BVHW04215305051
606632BV00020B/304